Luca's Scary Dream

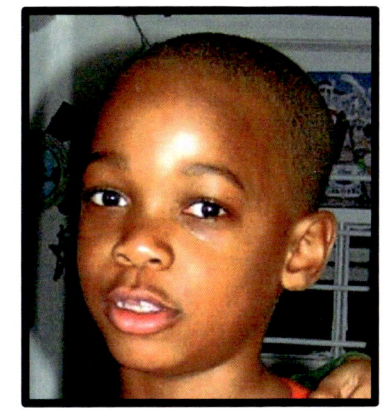

By MaryAnn McAlpin
Photos by James Napoli

"Anthony, are you awake?" whispered Luca.

"What's the matter?" asked Anthony.

"I had a scary dream!" said Luca.

"You did?" Anthony asked.

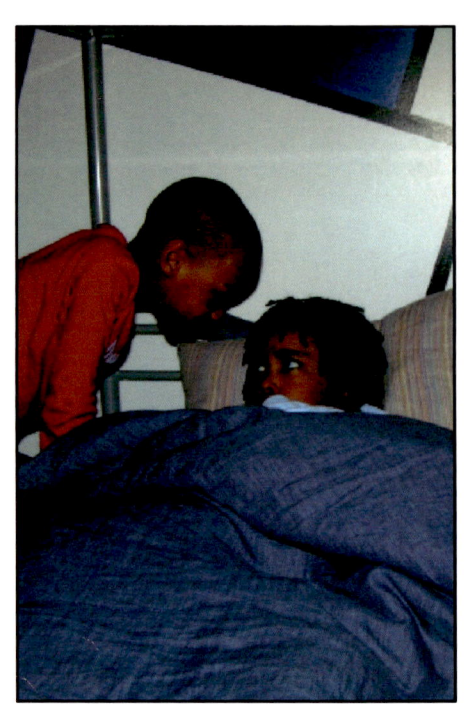

"Monsters were chasing me!" cried Luca. "I'm scared!"

"Oh no!" said Anthony.

"Now, I can't sleep," cried Luca.

"Maybe a glass of milk will help you go back to sleep," said Anthony.

"We can't get a glass of milk now," said Luca. "Dad is asleep."

"We can get it by ourselves," said Anthony. "We have to be very quiet!"

"OK," said Luca. "SHHHH!"

"Let's use our flashlight, so we don't have to turn on the lights," said Anthony.

"Good idea!" said Luca.

The boys went quietly down the stairs with the flashlight. They did **not** want to wake up Dad.

"Luca, what did the monsters in your dream look like?" asked Anthony.

"They were green and hairy with big noses," whispered Luca.

"Oooh! They must have been very scary monsters!" said Anthony. "You'll feel better after you get some milk."

"I hope so!" said Luca.

All of a sudden the boys heard a noise coming from the kitchen.

Who's there?

"Oh, no!" cried Luca. "I hope it's not the scary monsters!"

"SHHHH!" whispered Anthony. "It's OK, we can go look together!"

"DAD!" yelled both boys. "What are you doing here?"

"I had a scary dream and could not sleep!" said Dad. "What are you doing here?"

"Luca had a scary dream, too.
We want a glass of milk to help him feel better,"
said Anthony.

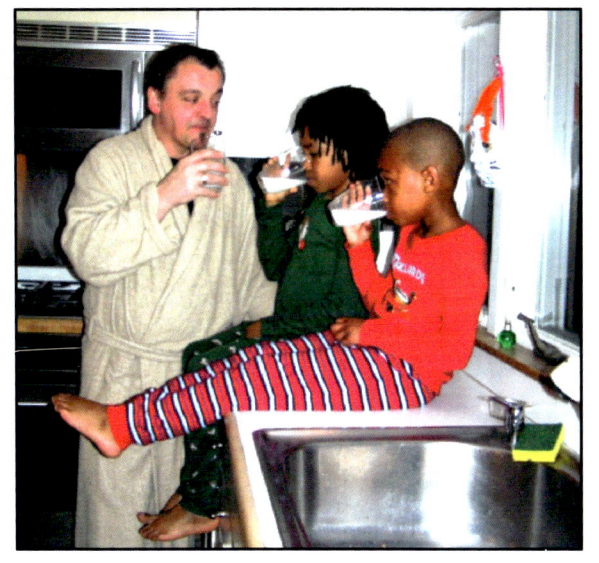

"That's a good idea," said Dad.
"We can all have a glass of milk and a cookie and talk about our dreams."

"Time to go back to bed, boys," said Dad.

"No more monsters!"